Look In

 # A Rabbit's Burrow

Rabbits make burrows
under the ground.
They dig many tunnels
with their strong
hind legs.

2

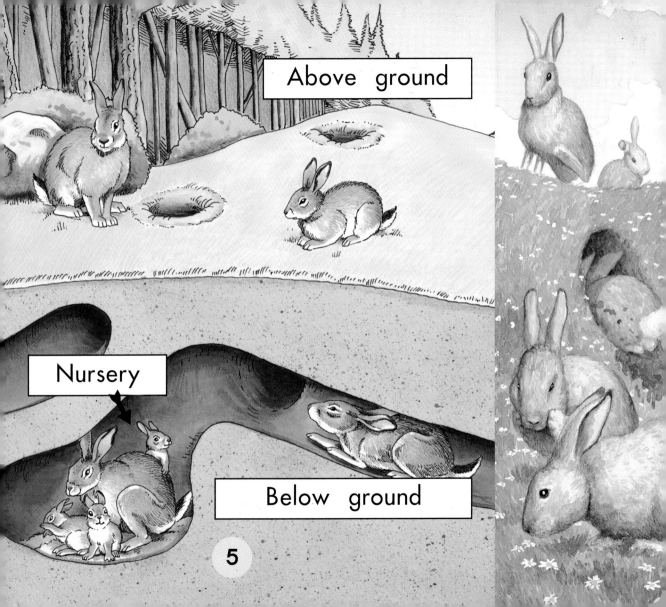

Above ground

Nursery

Below ground

5

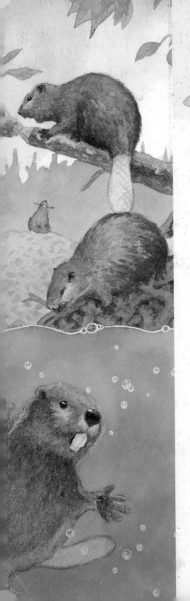

 # A Beaver's Lodge

Beavers make lodges
with sticks and logs.
They chew down trees
with their sharp teeth.

6

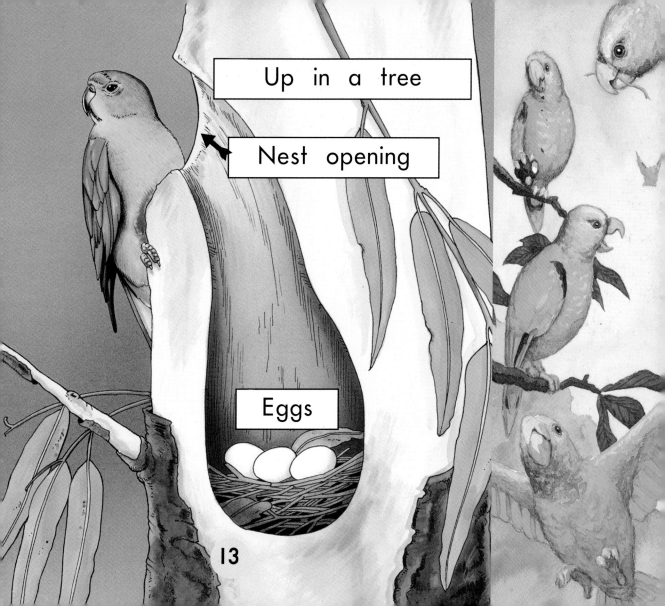

Up in a tree

Nest opening

Eggs

13

An Ant's Nest

Eggs and *larvae*

Anthill

Some ants make their nests under the ground or in mounds called anthills.

14

You can make
an ant nest.

You can watch
what happens
inside.

Glossary

chicks – baby parrots

kittens – baby rabbits

larvae – an early stage in the life of ants

pups – baby beavers